Made in the USA
Monee, IL
24 October 2021

80697505R00061